Books by Eric Hammel

76 Hours: The Invasion of Tarawa (with John E. Lane)
Chosin: Heroic Ordeal of the Korean War
The Root: The Marines in Beirut
Ace! A Marine Night-Fighter Pilot in World War II (with R. Bruce Porter)
Duel for the Golan (with Jerry Asher)
Guadalcanal: Starvation Island
Guadalcanal: The Carrier Battles
Guadalcanal: Decision at Sea
Munda Trail: The New Georgia Campaign
The Jolly Rogers (with Tom Blackburn)
Khe Sanh: Siege in the Clouds
First Across the Rhine (with David E. Pergrin)
Lima-6: A Marine Company Commander in Vietnam (with Richard D. Camp)
Ambush Valley
Fire in the Streets
Aces Against Japan
Aces Against Japan II
Aces Against Germany
Air War Europa: Chronology
Fire in the Streets
Carrier Clash
Aces at War
Air War Pacific: Chronology
Aces in Combat
Bloody Tarawa
Marines at War
Carrier Strike
Pacific Warriors: The U.S. Marines in World War II
Iwo Jima: Portrait of a Battle
Marines in Hue City: Portrait of an Urban Battle
The U.S. Marines in World War II: Guadalcanal
The U.S. Marines in World War II: New Georgia, Bougainville, and Cape Gloucester
The U.S. Marines in World War II: Tarawa and the Marshalls
How America Saved the World
Coral and Blood
The Road to Big Week
Islands of Hell
The Steel Wedge

ALWAYS FAITHFUL
U.S. Marines in World War II Combat

Eric Hammel

Designed by Tom Heffron

OSPREY
PUBLISHING

First published in Great Britain in 2011 by Osprey Publishing,
Midland House, West Way, Botley, Oxford, OX2 0PH, UK
44-02 23rd Street, Suite 219, Long Island City, NY 11101, USA
E-mail: info@ospreypublishing.com

OSPREY PUBLISHING IS PART OF THE OSPREY GROUP

A CIP catalogue record for this book is available from the British Library.

ISBN 978 1 84908 538 0

Jacket design and page layout by Tom Heffron, Hudson, Wisconsin, USA
Typeset in Adobe Caslon Pro
Originated by United Graphics Pte, Singapore
Printed in China through Bookbuilders

11 12 13 14 15   10 9 8 7 6 5 4 3 2 1

Osprey Publishing is supporting the Woodland Trust, the UK's leading
woodland conservation charity, by funding the dedication of trees.

www.ospreypublishing.com

Front Cover: Nancy Lee White Hoffman

Contents

Introduction

vii

1

Beach Assault

1

2

In the Jungle

25

3

Every Marine a Rifleman

49

4

Supporting Arms

61

5

In the Attack

73

6

Looking for a Fight

107

7

Stress and Tension

131

8

At Close Quarters

143

9

WIA

153

10

At Ease

171

11

The Fallen

191

12

Adieu

199

It is the war correspondent's job to find moments of truth on the battlefield, then to inscribe them in well-chosen words on the public consciousness. And it is on the same battlefield that combat photographers find moments of truth and inscribe them in searing images on the public psyche. The truths inscribed in the photographs in these pages are about human spirit, survival, thanksgiving, honor, brotherhood, and duty.

Introduction

During the first twenty-three months of the Pacific War, the United States Marine Corps devoted few resources to documenting the emerging war on film. Very few photographers were deployed to the Pacific, and they were neither trained nor often called upon to act as combat photographers. They were mostly former civilian news photographers assigned to create "feel good" publicity for the Marine Corps' recruiting efforts at home. They were tamped down, also, by national civilian leaders who feared that too much graphic truth from the front might further demoralize an American public already reeling from the horrors of Pearl Harbor, Wake, and the Philippines. The concept of "combat photographer"—the worldview, the name, and the training to go with it—did not really emerge in the field until November and December 1943, at Bougainville, Cape Gloucester, and Tarawa. The new concept coincided with the moment during which national civilian leaders themselves first realized that the rising tempo of the war, as it moved from defense to unremitting offense, would lead to dramatic increases in casualties for which the American people had not been adequately prepared. In late 1943, on viewing the first batch of brutally graphic battlefield photos brought to him fresh from the Tarawa battlefield, President Franklin Roosevelt decided on the spot that a nation so consumed by global war required a stiff dose of the truth. The first of these graphic battlefield photos appeared three weeks after they were taken, in the December 13, 1943, issue of *Life* Magazine. This was a risky move, but far from impinging on the national will, the bold truth-telling fortified American resolve, caused Americans at home and overseas to dig deeper into themselves, to produce more, to come together more, to crave victory more, to sacrifice more.

The photographic record that started so slowly and unevenly at Guadalcanal and on through the central Solomons perked up in November 1943, at both Bougainville and Tarawa, as more and better-organized photographers with a better idea about what to photograph moved into battle with Marine combat units. Thus the photographic record at this juncture became much larger and visibly mounted in intensity as Marines attacked time and again across the wide Pacific. The photos were of better quality—more immediate, more sympathetic—toward the combat Marines who had to assault the beaches, brave the fire, endure the bombardments, take the hills, comb the valleys and forests, and reduce all manner of Japanese defensive schemes that marked the long, long road to victory.

As well, the photos became more knowing and more insightful as the photographers increasingly shared the day-to-day, moment-by-moment, life-and-death struggles their combatant comrades had been thrown into. Indeed, as the photographers put more battle experience under their own belts, they became more hard-bitten—more fatalistic and less cautious, yet more willing to come to grips with the many faces of war that expressed themselves everywhere they pointed their camera lenses, as other young men fought and died on the shared battlefield, in the shared state of privation.

Over time, the photographers and the photographic record they created became surpassingly faithful to the Marines who took the risks to win the battles. And now, as that generation slips away, the photos alone remain faithful as an immutable historical record of that time and for all time.

Every now and then, through the application of bravery, knowledge of war, or just plain luck, Marine combat photographers captured moments that, for their insight into human nature alone, can be confidently referred to as "art." This volume, then, is, hopefully not perversely, a study of art painted on a canvas of willful suffering.

A number of the photographs in this book are considered iconic by several generations of U.S. Marines. These icons could not be left out of this collection simply because they might be too familiar. Indeed, they are the touchstones that make these selections from among many thousands of combat photos all the more telling because they provide a benchmark and touch a level of awareness my own selections must match or exceed.

I give great credence to the old saw that a photo is worth a thousand words. Each selection in these pages is offered without explanation of any sort. Only a place and time caption appears with each photo. Yet, though words are not used, each photograph is instantly recognizable as a complete message, as a moment of truth and humanity. And the message grows longer and more familiar as the eye lingers and drills down to bedrock details that humans instinctively gather from other humans without the exchange of a single word: from the set of a chin, from posture, from the cast of an eye, from a whole range of human nonverbal shorthand.

So, except to provide the context of a place and a date—and except for this introduction—the photos in this volume speak their truths all by themselves; only you can hear those truths, only you can draw the lessons they offer.

Eric Hammel, Northern California, Winter 2010

Roi Island, Kwajalein Atoll

—

January 31–February 2, 1944

1

BEACH ASSAULT

It was always the same. New troops heading to first combat believed reports that the prelanding bombardment had defeated the Japanese before the first Marine set foot ashore. The assault troops, veteran and novice alike, dutifully stormed the beach, but caution set in whether or not they were under fire. And when the Japanese fire inevitably commenced, the assault froze as leaders and followers ducked down to assess the immediate situation.

Meanwhile, problems mounted. Because of overcrowding behind whatever cover and concealment the inland verges of the beach afforded, it became difficult to land more troops, ammunition, or other supplies. This led to congestion at the surf line, and that threw off the schedules the supply-laden vehicles and landing craft had been called on to meet. So in addition to damaged amphibian tractors and landing craft taken out of service while the beaches were uncongested, tractors and landing craft caught in traffic jams with sorely needed follow-on troops and supplies were not only slowed, they also were made more vulnerable to defensive fires for longer than was worth the risk of whatever their crews thought they could accomplish.

And then—as has always happened in Marine Corps history—a sparkplug ignited the stalled engine of war. A troop leader—a sergeant or a lieutenant—or perhaps a teenage private with command presence decided that his honor was at stake, or that it was dumber to be a sitting, passive target than a moving, aggressive warrior. So he stood up and hurled an order or a challenge to all who could hear: "Follow me!" And because many of those other men felt that their own honor or manhood had been compromised, the mindset they had been brutally drilled to attain kicked back in, and suddenly a gaggle of timid individuals was transformed into a fully integrated machine made for taking war to the enemy.

Some men never advanced under fire, but, somehow, all who would be needed did. And, then, victory was just a matter of time.

New Britain

—

December 26, 1944–April 1944

Guam

July 21–August 11, 1944

Iwo Jima

—

February 19–March 16, 1945

Iwo Jima

February 19–March 16, 1945

Saipan

—

June 15–July 9, 1944

Saipan

—

June 15–July 9, 1944

Iwo Jima

—

February 19–March 16, 1945

Bougainville

—

November 1, 1943–January 16, 1944

Saipan

—

June 15–July 9, 1944

Tarawa

November 19–23, 1943

Tarawa

—

November 19–23, 1943

New Britain

—

December 26, 1943–April 1944

2

IN THE JUNGLE

Most of the island battlefields the Marines encountered in the Pacific featured densely wooded areas, but the early South Pacific campaigns—Guadalcanal, New Georgia, Bougainville, and New Britain—were fought almost entirely in interminable, close rain-forest settings the Marines called "the jungle." The environment itself overwhelmed the senses with crippling heat compounded by strength-sapping humidity. Noise from falling trees and moving but invisible wildlife further crowded the senses. Vistas were rare and limited. Each step might bring a Marine into the gunsight of a patient Japanese sniper, or cause one to tumble into any of a hundred dangerous obstacles, or become mired in mud so deep and viscous as to trap a strong man unless his comrades could pull him to safety. Even where action was sporadic, the sheer enormity of the close rain forest and the awful variety of the dangers it presented—disease, depression, disorientation, falling trees and branches, and much more—sapped the intellect, slowed the reflexes, overwhelmed the senses, and stressed body and soul for weeks and even months on end.

There were few compensations for the unrelieved suffering, few kills scored for the incessant burden of hunting game that hunted back. The Japanese moved or waited in silence while Marines advanced slowly, carefully as all the senses they could muster—sound, sight, smell, even clairvoyance—were deployed to scan in all directions at all times. Sometimes the Japanese showed themselves in mass attacks, but most often they could not be perceived but for fleeting glimpses or the accumulated wisdom of one's hypersensitive instincts.

Bougainville

—

November 1, 1943–January 16, 1944

Bougainville

——

November 1, 1943–January 16, 1944

Bougainville

—

November 1, 1943–January 16, 1944

Bougainville

November 1, 1943–January 16, 1944

Bougainville

—

November 1, 1943–January 16, 1944

New Britain

—

December 26, 1943–April 1944

Bougainville

—

November 1, 1943–January 16, 1944

Bougainville

—

November 1, 1943–January 16, 1944

New Britain

December 26, 1943–April 1944

Guadalcanal

—

August 7, 1942–February 9, 1943

Okinawa

—

April 1–June 22, 1945

3

EVERY MARINE A RIFLEMAN

The Marine Corps is a proud organization with many proud traditions. One of its proudest traditions and foremost characteristics is that every Marine, regardless of his specific job, is a rifleman above all. Even pilots—and combat photographers—must qualify with a rifle.

By mid-1943, Marine infantrymen were equipped with the world's leading common infantry rifle, the eight-shot semiautomatic .30-06-caliber Garand M1. In well-trained hands, the M1 was extremely accurate at any range. Other shoulder weapons Marines brought to Pacific battlefields included the less-powerful, shorter-range .30-06-caliber M1 and M2 semiautomatic carbine favored by typically heavily burdened machine-gun and mortar crewmen and ammunition carriers; and the Browning Automatic Rifle (BAR), also a .30-06-caliber weapon that provided Marine infantry squads and fire teams with accurate, long-range supporting fire. Fired in single-shot mode, the BAR doubled as an awesomely accurate ad hoc sniper rifle at very long ranges. In short supply until late in the war, the famous .45-caliber Thompson submachine gun (Tommygun) was excellent for close-in fighting but inaccurate at ranges beyond fifty yards. Marines, especially troop leaders and members of machine-gun and mortar squads, also qualified with the .45-caliber Colt M1911A1 semiautomatic pistol, which, like the Tommygun, was accurate only at short range.

It often is difficult, in the throes of life-or-death combat, for even the best-trained rifleman to calm down sufficiently to fall back on the mantra and actions that characterized his earliest training as a rifleman: breathe–release–squeeze. Trained Marine snipers were rare on Pacific island battlefields, but if the moment is right and the opportunity is there, every Marine has it in him to become a deadly accurate sniper.

Iwo Jima

—

February 19–March 16, 1945

Guam

—

July 21–August 11, 1944

Saipan

—

June 15–July 9, 1944

Bougainville

—

November 1, 1943–January 16, 1944

4

SUPPORTING ARMS

Amphibious warfare in the Pacific relied most heavily upon infantrymen, armored in their cloth shirts, who faced dug-in Japanese infantrymen at close quarters. But the Marine Corps was a completely modern war-fighting organization that fielded a completely modern range of weapons, including artillery adapted to an amphibious role, mortars, antitank guns (good for busting bunkers), tanks, and even an air force that became heavily invested in providing close support for Marines on the ground. Wherever Marine riflemen went, Marine supporting arms went with them.

Saipan

June 15–July 9, 1944

Guam

—

July 21–August 11, 1944

Guadalcanal

—

August 7, 1942–February 9, 1943

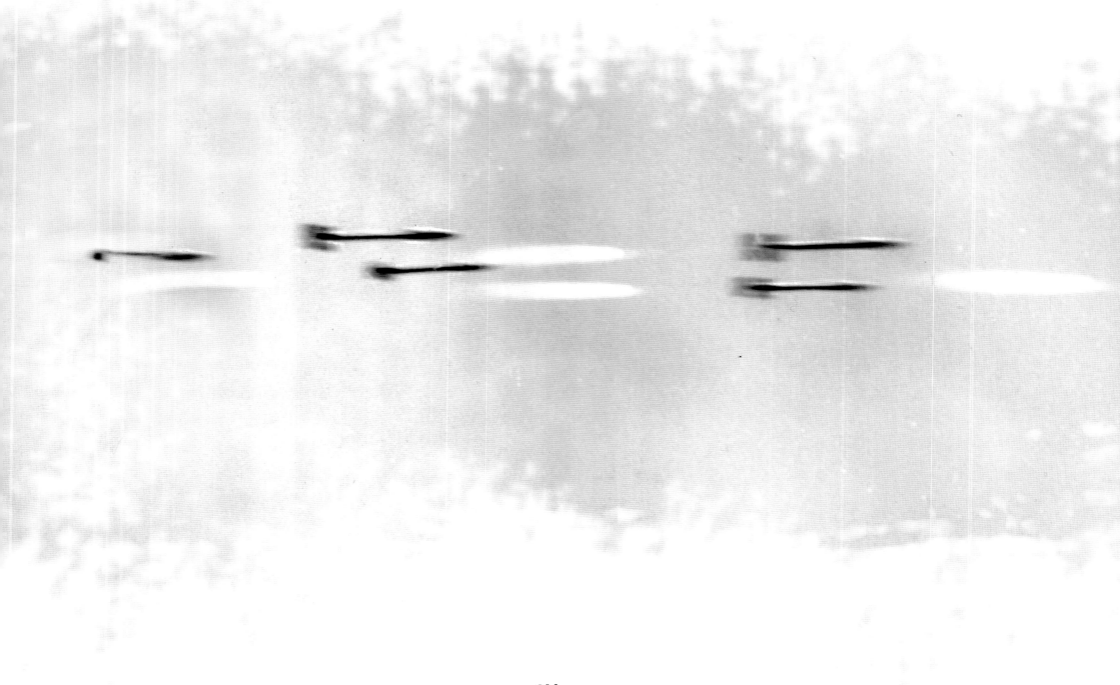

Okinawa

—

April 1–June 22, 1945

Tinian

—

July 24–August 1, 1944

Iwo Jima

—

February 19–March 16, 1945

5

IN THE ATTACK

All the planning and maneuvering in the world, all the artillery and air bombardment possible, all the training absorbed, and all the inherent bravery a man can possess always come down to a moment of truth. To achieve victory on any battlefield in all of history, one side or the other has to get up and go—has to *attack*; has to close with the enemy; has to kill enemy soldiers or send them fleeing; has to prevail; has to take possession of the enemy's defensive works or his camp, town, city, or countryside.

Eniwetok Atoll

—

February 17–March 2, 1944

Iwo Jima

—

February 19–March 16, 1945

New Britain

—

December 26, 1943–April 1944

Saipan

—

June 15–July 9, 1944

Iwo Jima

February 19–March 16, 1945

Tarawa

—

November 20–23, 1943

Okinawa

—

April 1–June 22, 1945

Saipan

—

June 15–July 9, 1945

Iwo Jima

—

February 19–March 16, 1945

Saipan

—

June 15–July 9, 1944

Iwo Jima

—

February 19–March 16, 1945

Saipan

—

June 15–July 9, 1944

Okinawa

—

April 1–June 22, 1945

Okinawa

—

April 1–June 22, 1945

6

LOOKING FOR A FIGHT

The Marine Corps of World War II trained for a war of movement, a war of rapid blunt-force advances—one after another, from intermediate goal to intermediate goal—a war of conquest in the shortest possible time. The dominant theory was that fewer casualties resulted from blunt-force, persistent aggression than from the slower, more deliberate war of attrition favored by most traditional armies of the day. In practical terms suited to the kind of warfare it faced in the Pacific, the Marine Corps doctrine, and the ethos it fostered, meant that Marines on the front line were always looking to take it to the enemy, always looking for a fight.

Saipan

—

June 15–July 9, 1944

Okinawa

—

April 1–June 22, 1945

Saipan
—
June 15–July 9, 1944

Okinawa

—

April 1–June 22, 1945

Saipan

—

June 15–July 9, 1944

Iwo Jima

—

February 19–March 16, 1945

Saipan

—

June 15–July 9, 1944

Peleliu

—

September 15–October 15, 1944

Okinawa
—
April 1–June 22, 1945

Saipan

—

June 15–July 9, 1944

7

STRESS AND TENSION

Marines are human. Their rigorous training to fight aggressively and their constant immersion in the warrior ethos do much to set them apart, but Marines are human. They feel pain. They know fear. They feel uncertainty. See it on their faces, their perfectly human faces, and in body language that mirrors the thoughts any human would conjure in a life-or-death fight. To be a Marine in combat alongside other Marines is about being human, then overcoming the shackles imposed by merely being human.

Stress and tension are good. They heighten the senses, they enhance the hunt. They are overcome by falling back on training, by trusting in the organization, by giving oneself wholly to the enterprise. Stress and tension encourage a Marine to focus on the job at hand.

Peleliu

—

September 15–October 15, 1944

Saipan

—

June 15–July 9, 1944

Iwo Jima

—

February 19–March 16, 1945

Peleliu

—

September 15–October 15, 1944

8

AT CLOSE QUARTERS

At root, there's only one of two ways to win: kill the enemy or drive him to surrender. And, at root, there's only one way to kill the enemy: get close enough so that one weapon or another—from 16-inch naval guns to 2,000-pound bombs, from bayonets to five strong fingers—can be brought to bear. And so it goes: overcome doubt and fear, stress and tension; attack; bring it to the enemy; get close enough to force his hands to signal surrender; or just plain kill him. Brutal, but simple. If there has to be war at all, it must in its essence boil down to these brutal, simple tenets.

Saipan

———

June 15–July 9, 1944

Okinawa

—

April 1–June 22, 1945

Tarawa

—

November 20–23, 1943

Tarawa

—

November 20–23, 1943

9

WIA

United States Marines have always seen the recovery, evacuation, and treatment of wounded and injured comrades as one of the sacred definitions of battlefield honor. When a Marine or Navy hospital corpsman serving with Marines says "Semper Fi" to anyone, he means, "I will risk my life, endure any hardship, to save yours."

To achieve the sacred trust that no one will be willingly left behind, that the injured will be succored and lives will be saved, the U.S. Navy and Marine Corps in World War II expended large swathes of training and treasure on casualty treatment and evacuation. Front-line Navy hospital corpsmen were easily recognized, even when wearing the same jungle utility uniforms as Marines, by the Unit-1 aid bag they carried, an over-the-shoulder pack filled with the essential supplies needed to administer front-line first aid. Many front-line Marines also carried medical supply packets and bandages, but only the "docs" could carry or administer morphine. Front-line medicine had few goals: triage, control of the bleeding, and fending off deadly shock. Higher scales of treatment were reserved for medical aid echelons behind the front lines: physician-manned aid stations at the battalion and regimental levels, evacuation hospitals at the division level, bigger and more elaborate hospitals and hospital ships farther back, and as far afield as military general hospitals in American cities.

Saipan

—

June 15–July 9, 1944

Saipan

—

June 15–July 9, 1944

Okinawa

—

April 15–June 22, 1945

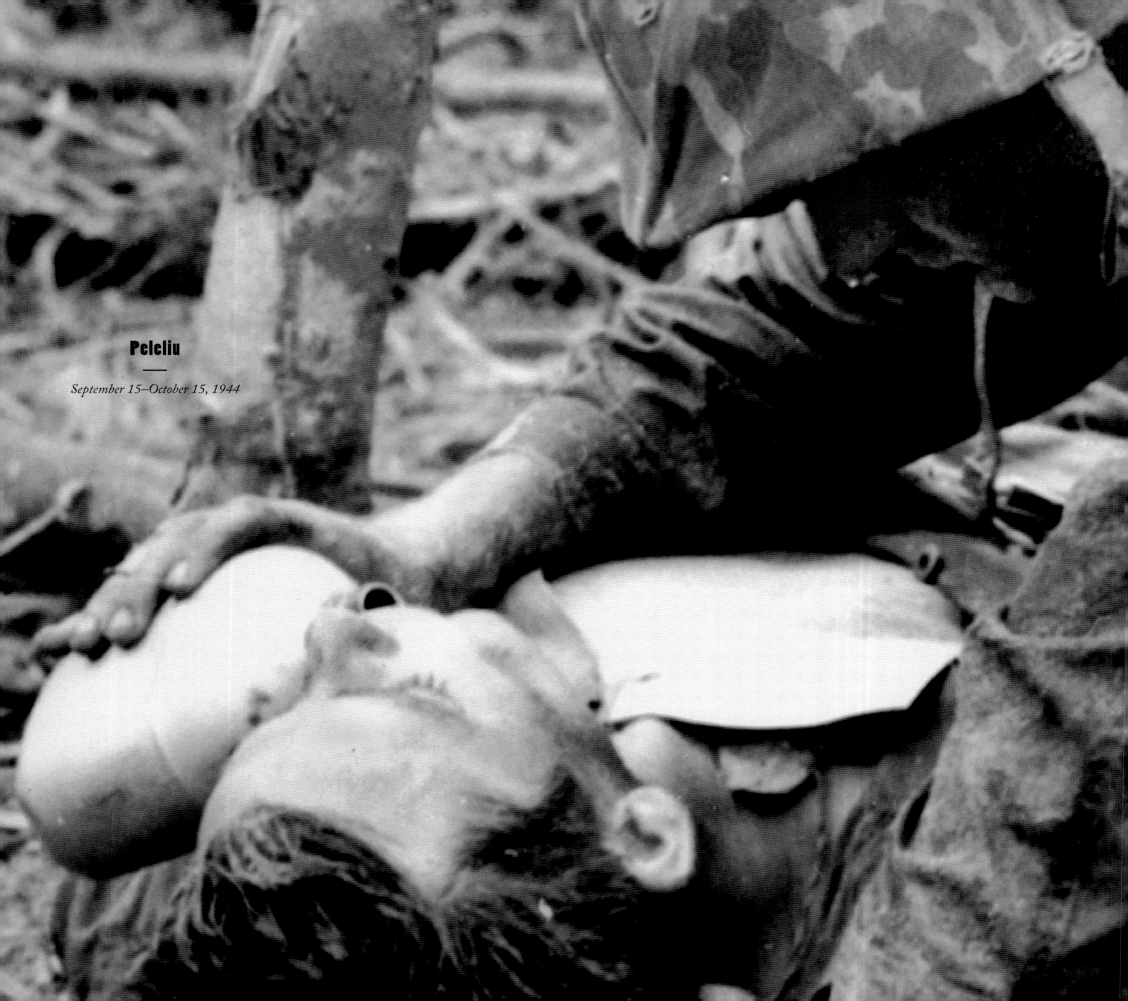

Peleliu

—

September 15–October 15, 1944

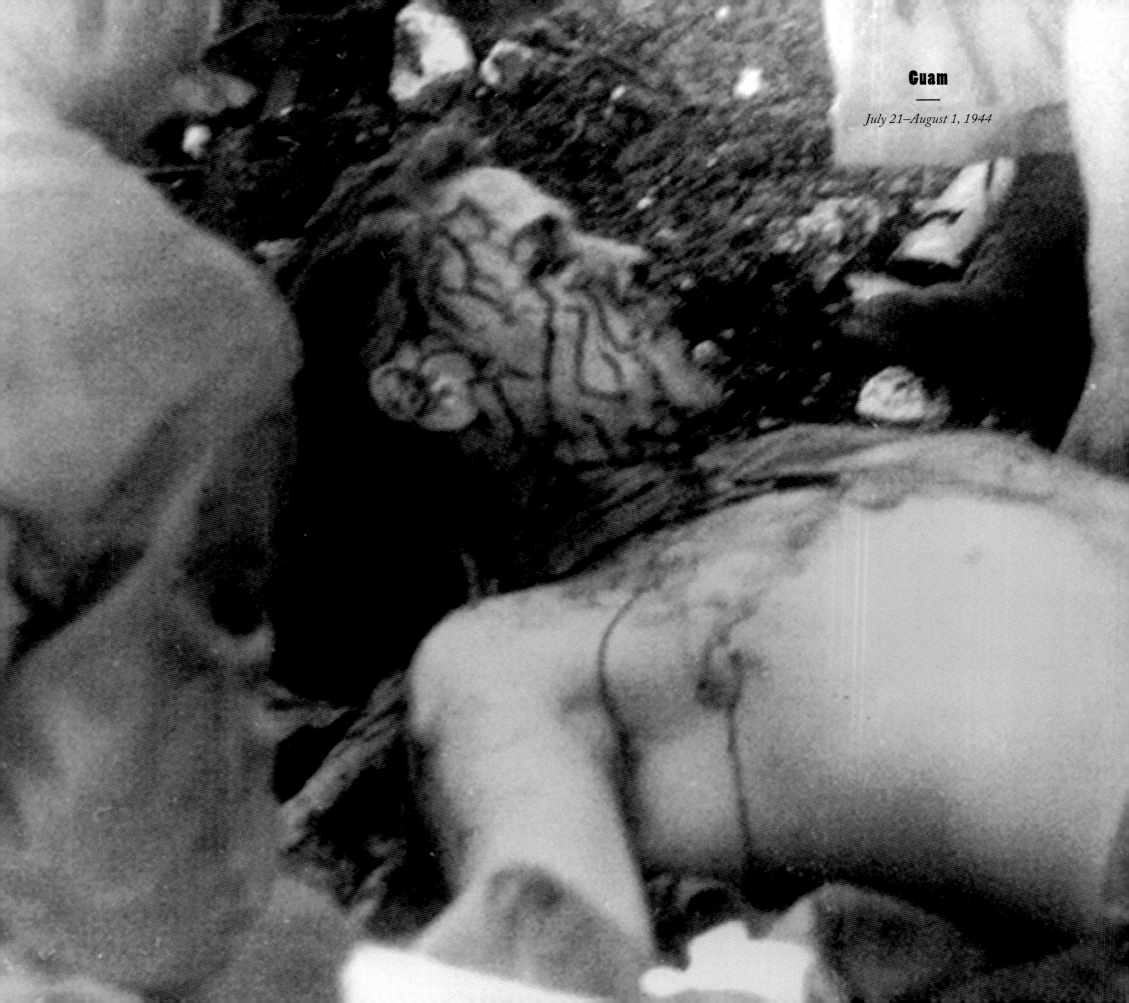

Eniwetok Atoll

—

February 19–24, 1944

Iwo Jima

—

February 19–March 16, 1945

Iwo Jima

—

February 19–March 16, 1945

Guam

—

July 21–August 11, 1944

10

AT EASE

Though trained to get by on very little sleep and amped by all the fear-induced adrenalin their bodies could produce, even young Marines required a little time off now and then to pull themselves together. On or near the battlefield, their repose speaks of vigilance. On their faces are the first signs of hauntings that would follow those who survived into old age.

Iwo Jima

February 19–March 16, 1945

Saipan

—

June 15–July 9, 1944

Iwo Jima

—

February 19–March 16, 1945

Okinawa

—

April 1–June 22, 1945

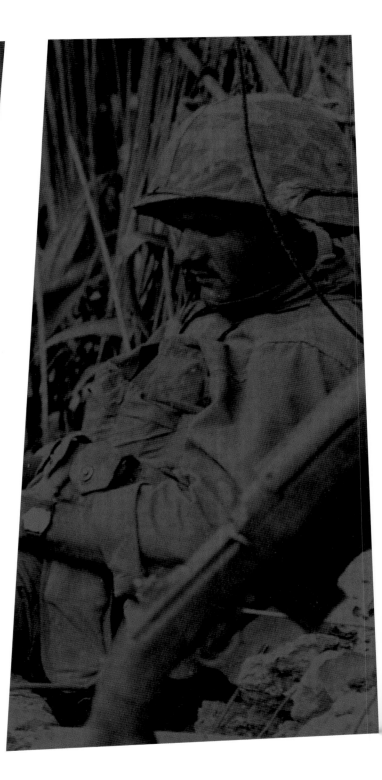

Iwo Jima

—

February 19–March 16, 1945

Tinian

—

July 24–August 1, 1944

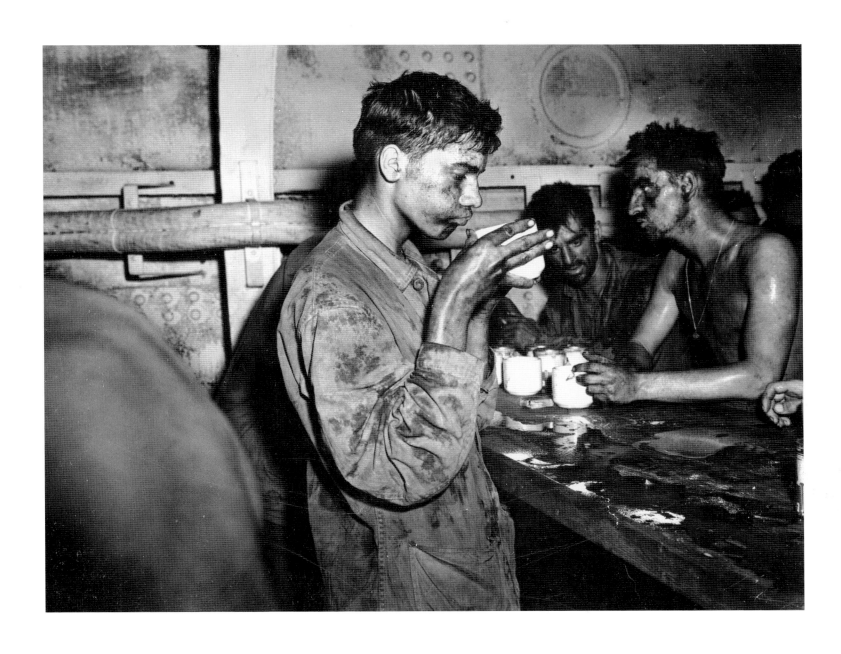

New Britain

—

December 26, 1943–April 1944

11

THE FALLEN

And when he gets to Heaven,
To Saint Peter he will tell,
"One more Marine reporting, sir.
I've served my time in Hell."

—Anonymous

*Found on a battlefield grave
on Guadalcanal*

Bougainville

November 1, 1943–January 16, 1944

Saipan

June 15–July 9, 1944

Iwo Jima

February 19–March 16, 1945

Okinawa

—

April 1–June 22, 1945

12

ADIEU

'Til the last landing's made,
and we stand unafraid
on a shore no mortal has seen,
'til the last bugle call
sounds Taps for us all,
it's "Semper Fidelis, Marine."